Copyright ©2021 by Yunetta Spring Smith

All rights reserved. No part of the publication may be reproduced, distributed, or transmitted in any form or by any means, including photocopying, recording, or other electronic or mechanical methods, without the prior written consent of the publisher, except in the case of brief quotations in a reviews and certain other noncommercial uses permitted by copyright law. For permission requests, write to the publisher, at the address below:

MAILING ADDRESS
P.O. Box 3801
Clarksville, TN 37043

EMAIL ADDRESS
GroundBreakersc.c@gmail.com

PHONE NUMBER
931-338-8882

ISBN: 978-0-578-25438-8

Take the Struggle out of Self-Care/6 Weeks to Create your Self-Care Strategy
Electronic workbook
Template Designer: Miri Campbell
Editor: Dynioua Negrón-León
Photography by Elle Danielle
Location The Russell Boutique Hotel Nashville tn

STAY CONNECTED WITH YUNETTA

Website: Springforthcounseling.org groundbreakerstherapy.com
Linktree: linktr.ee/yunettaspring01
Facebook: @springforthcounseling @yunettaspring
Instagram: @springforthcounseling @yunettaspring @groundbreakerstherapy
YouTube: @Yunettaspring

This workbook is dedicated to my mother and the girl.

Ma, Thank you for caring for me when you couldn't always care for yourself. Your sacrifices have never gone unnoticed and will forever be appreciated. Thank you for carrying me until I was able to stand on my own two feet. I hope that these words will empower someone to stand on theirs as well. Your love, compassion, and care has shaped me into the woman I am today. I hope you continue to experience the warmth of all the love you continuously give.

To my daughter thank you for being the most "beautifulist" girl in this world! You are my biggest motivation and motivator. You are one of kind. Fearfully and wonderfully made. You bring me joy in more ways than you can imagine. I'm so proud of the young lady you are blooming to be. Keep blooming unapologetically.

Love You Mean It

WELCOME

Hello Beautiful People

I am so excited that you have made the decision to go on this self-care journey with me. It is my hope that this manual will enhance your Awareness, increase your Accountability, and Activate your desire for Action.

Yunetta Spring

Before we start, jot down your intentions for taking the course and imagine what you hope to achieve.

CHECK IN

Before we get into this course I want you to do a quick self evaluation. Rate your present self care practices below. No Shade. No Shame. No Blame. Just Reflect.

RATING SCALE

0 — RARELY TRUE
1 — SOMETIMES TRUE
2 — OFTEN TRUE

1. I feel confident in my daily self-care practice _____
2. I have a tendency to care for others before myself _____
3. I have a tendency to ignore my personal needs _____
4. I feel tired on most days _____
5. When my day is complete I feel fulfilled _____
6. I can recognize how and when to set boundaries _____
7. I have a tendency to overextend myself _____
8. I feel satisfied with the reciprocity in my relationships _____
9. When I am overwhelmed I ask for help _____
10. I feel guilty when I can't show up for others _____

☐ **MODULE 1** — You can't know where you're going unless you first know where you are

☐ **MODULE 2** — You cannot heal if you are unwilling to feel

☐ **MODULE 3** — Begin with the end in mind

☐ **MODULE 4** — If you fail to plan you plan to fail

☐ **MODULE 5** — It's Time for some action

☐ **MODULE 6** — You can't lose if you learn

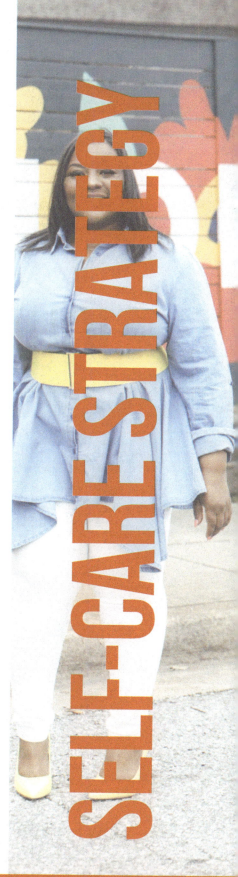

SELF-CARE STRATEGY

JOURNAL PROMPTS

What is Self-Care?   08

Who taught you how to care for yourself?   22

It's hard to care for myself because?   37

Write about a time when you felt cared for?   49

What has been your greatest accomplishment?   66

How has your perspective of self care changed?   79

MODULE ONE

You can't know where your going unless you first know where you are." In this module you will identify what self care is. You will take a glance at your day and rate your current self care practices. Hold on this isn't the time to take action or make adjustments just notice.

MODULE ONE

In this module you will learn:

- How to communicate your definition of self care.

- The 10 Various types of self-care.

- How you view and manage your time on a daily and weekly basis.

- How much time and energy you give to others.

- What activities consume more of your time and attention.

Journal Time
WHAT IS SELF-CARE?

TYPES OF SELF-CARE

Below you will find different types of self-care. Check the boxes you engage in often.

☐ *PHYSICAL*

☐ *EMOTIONAL*

☐ *SOCIAL*

☐ *SPIRITUAL*

☐ *PERSONAL*

TYPES OF SELF-CARE

Below you will find different types of self-care. Check the boxes you engage in often.

☐ FINANCIAL

☐ PROFESSIONAL

☐ ENVIRONMENTAL

☐ SPATIAL

☐ SKIN CARE

10 TYPES OF SELF CARE

There are so many ways you can care for yourself. Check out the various forms of self care and the descriptions below. Identify the different ways you are already doing a great job caring for yourself.

PHYSICAL

Physical self-care involves activities that improve physical health and well-being.
Ex. Drinking Water, Getting More Sleep,
and Exercise.

EMOTIONAL

The purpose of emotional self-care is to learn how to control your emotions and lifting yourself up when you feel down.
Ex. Therapy, Journaling, or Activities to Express Your Feelings.

SOCIAL

Activities that develop and deepen relationships with the people in your life.
Ex. Calling Family Regularly or Brunch with Friends.

SPIRITUAL

Spiritual Self-Care doesn't have to be religious, although it sometimes is. This self-care includes activities to stimulate your mind and allows you to think bigger.
Ex. Going to Church, Meditation, or Yoga.

MENTAL

Mental self-care is about relaxing and keeping your stress low. It's about stimulating your brain and remaining positive.
Ex. Meditation, Reading Books, or Solving a Puzzle.

SPATIAL

Protecting your space, keeping your distince in public settings. Designating a space specifically designed for self-care.

10 TYPES OF SELF CARE

There are so many ways you can care for yourself. Check out the various forms of self care and the descriptions below. Identify the different ways you are already doing a great job caring for you. Add two additional forms of self-care.

FINANCIAL

Developing Habits that Work for You and Reflecting what you're trying to achieve with your money.
Ex. Review Bank Accounts, Budgets, and Create Financial Goals.

PROFESSIONAL

This is self-care related to your work life. It includes reducing stress in your career, acquiring practices to create a work-life balance.

ENVIRONMENTAL

Keeping your work and home organized, while understanding what in your enviroment is important to you.
Ex. Playing with Pets and Family, Clean Home, and Enjoy Nature.

SKIN CARE

Awareness of the products you use. Refraining from harmful chemicals. Identifying what you put on your skin and being intentional about staying away from toxic or harmful ingredients.

TOP PRIORITY TO DO LIST FOR THE WEEK

IDENTIFY YOUR TOP 10 PRIORITIES FOR THE WEEK. THEN INDICATE IF THE LISTED TASKS ARE FOR YOURSELF OR OTHERS.

TASK　　　　　　　　　　　　　　　　　　　SELF / OTHERS

☐ _____　　_____
☐ _____　　_____
☐ _____　　_____
☐ _____　　_____
☐ _____　　_____
☐ _____　　_____
☐ _____　　_____
☐ _____　　_____
☐ _____　　_____
☐ _____　　_____

RANK WHAT TASKS "FEEL" MOST IMPORTANT.

1. _____

2. _____

3. _____

YOUR DAY YOUR WAY

DAY 1 WEEK 1 ACTIVITY LOG

SELF-CARE
Ain't selfish

What types of self care did you engaged in today?

PHYSICAL
EMOTIONAL
SOCIAL
SPIRITUAL
PERSONAL
SPATIAL
FINANCIAL
PROFESSIONAL
ENVIRONMENTAL
SKIN CARE

Rate your self-care 1-10

YOUR DAY YOUR WAY

DAY 2 WEEK 1 ACTIVITY LOG

SELF-CARE
Ain't selfish

What types of self care did you engaged in today?

PHYSICAL
EMOTIONAL
SOCIAL
SPIRITUAL
PERSONAL
SPATIAL
FINANCIAL
PROFESSIONAL
ENVIRONMENTAL
SKIN CARE

Rate your self-care 1-10

YOUR DAY YOUR WAY

DAY 3 WEEK 1 ACTIVITY LOG

SELF-CARE
Ain't selfish

What types of self care did you engaged in today?

PHYSICAL
EMOTIONAL
SOCIAL
SPIRITUAL
PERSONAL
SPATIAL
FINANCIAL
PROFESSIONAL
ENVIRONMENTAL
SKIN CARE

Rate your self-care 1-10

YOUR DAY YOUR WAY

DAY 4 WEEK 1 ACTIVITY LOG

SELF-CARE
Ain't selfish

What types of self care did you engaged in today?

PHYSICAL
EMOTIONAL
SOCIAL
SPIRITUAL
PERSONAL
SPATIAL
FINANCIAL
PROFESSIONAL
ENVIRONMENTAL
SKIN CARE

Rate your self-care 1-10

YOUR DAY YOUR WAY

DAY 5 WEEK 1 ACTIVITY LOG

SELF-CARE
Ain't selfish

What types of self care did you engaged in today?

PHYSICAL
EMOTIONAL
SOCIAL
SPIRITUAL
PERSONAL
SPATIAL
FINANCIAL
PROFESSIONAL
ENVIRONMENTAL
SKIN CARE

Rate your self-care 1-10

CULTIVATING CLARITY

Take some time and reflect over the past week. Think about your self-care practices and ask yourself the following questions...

How would you describe your self-care practices?

What experiences did you enjoy this week?

What experiences did you find to be challenging?

How would you describe your relationship with yourself?

When do you feel relaxed and rested?

When are you productive and focused?

MODULE TWO

"You cannot heal if you are unwilling to feel". In this section you will check your feelings. This isn't an attempt to judge or change your feelings just notice them throughout the day. Do you recognize any patterns? Write it out.

MODULE TWO

In this module you will learn:

- How to define feelings.

- How our feelings can impair, inform, and empower us.

- How have you been conditioned to view and manage your feelings?

- What activities do you engage in when you feel unpleasant and uncomfortable feelings?

- How often and how do you sit with your feelings?

Journal Time
WHO TAUGHT YOU HOW TO CARE FOR YOURSELF?

FEELING CHART

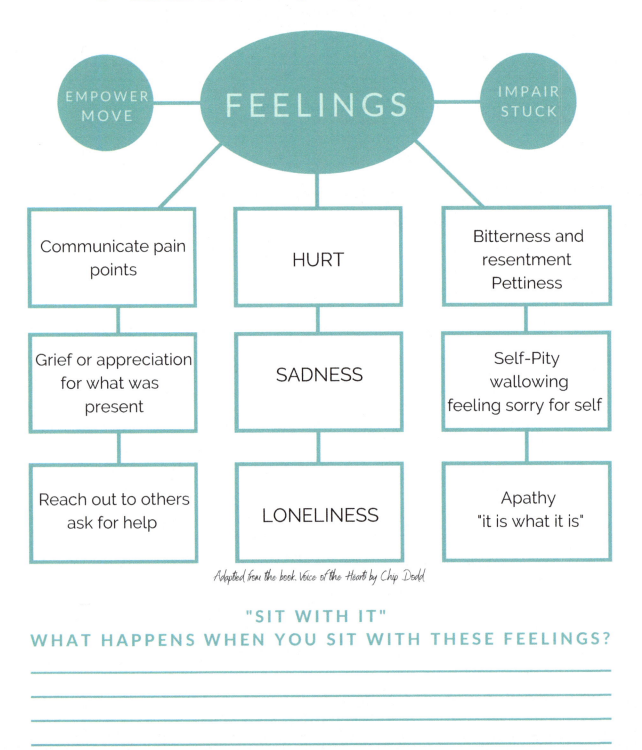

Adapted from the book, Voice of the Heart by Chip Dodd

"SIT WITH IT"
WHAT HAPPENS WHEN YOU SIT WITH THESE FEELINGS?

_____
_____
_____
_____

FEELING CHART

Adapted from the book, Voice of the Heart by Chip Dodd

"SIT WITH IT"
WHAT HAPPENS WHEN YOU SIT WITH THESE FEELINGS?

_____
_____
_____
_____

FEELING CHART

Adapted from the book, Voice of the Heart by Chip Dodd

"SIT WITH IT"
WHAT HAPPENS WHEN YOU SIT WITH THESE FEELINGS?

_____
_____
_____
_____

UNPACK YOUR FEELINGS

Take a moment to describe your experience with the feelings below. Think about a significant encounter with this feeling. Identify how you expressed this feeling.

DIG DEEPER
Consider various ways your parents, caretakers, or family members expressed their feelings as well.

HURT

SADNESS

LONELINESS

UNPACK YOUR FEELINGS

Take a moment to describe your experience with the feelings below. Think about a significant encounter with this feeling. Identify how you expressed this feeling.

DIG DEEPER
Consider various ways your parents, caretakers, or family members expressed their feelings as well.

FEAR

ANGER

SHAME

UNPACK YOUR FEELINGS

Take a moment to describe your experience with the feelings below. Think about a significant encounter with this feeling. Identify how you expressed this feeling.

DIG DEEPER
Consider various ways your parents, caretakers, or family members expressed their feelings as well.

GUILT

GLADNESS

HOPEFULNESS

YOUR DAY YOUR WAY

DAY 1 WEEK 2 ACTIVITY LOG

SELF-CARE
Act of love

What types of self care did you engaged in today?

PHYSICAL
EMOTIONAL
SOCIAL
SPIRITUAL
PERSONAL
SPATIAL
FINANCIAL
PROFESSIONAL
ENVIRONMENTAL
SKIN CARE

Rate your self-care 1-10

YOUR DAY YOUR WAY

DAY 2 WEek 2 ACTIVITY LOG

SELF-CARE
Act of love

What types of self care did you engaged in today?

PHYSICAL
EMOTIONAL
SOCIAL
SPIRITUAL
PERSONAL
SPATIAL
FINANCIAL
PROFESSIONAL
ENVIRONMENTAL
SKIN CARE

Rate your self-care 1-10

YOUR DAY YOUR WAY

DAY 3 WEEK 2 ACTIVITY LOG

SELF-CARE
Act of love

What types of self care did you engaged in today?

PHYSICAL
EMOTIONAL
SOCIAL
SPIRITUAL
PERSONAL
SPATIAL
FINANCIAL
PROFESSIONAL
ENVIRONMENTAL
SKIN CARE

Rate your self-care 1-10

YOUR DAY YOUR WAY

DAY 4 WEEK 2 ACTIVITY LOG

SELF-CARE
Act of love

What types of self care did you engaged in today?

PHYSICAL
EMOTIONAL
SOCIAL
SPIRITUAL
PERSONAL
SPATIAL
FINANCIAL
PROFESSIONAL
ENVIRONMENTAL
SKIN CARE

Rate your self-care 1-10

YOUR DAY YOUR WAY

DAY 5 WEEK 2 ACTIVITY LOG

SELF-CARE
Act of love

What types of self care did you engaged in today?

PHYSICAL
EMOTIONAL
SOCIAL
SPIRITUAL
PERSONAL
SPATIAL
FINANCIAL
PROFESSIONAL
ENVIRONMENTAL
SKIN CARE

Rate your self-care 1-10

CULTIVATING CLARITY

Take some time and reflect over the past week. Ask yourself the following questions...

What have you noticed about your feelings this week?

What feelings do you notice more?

What feelings did you find to be a challenge?

What are your thoughts about the feeling chart?

Do you feel stuck or are you moving through your feelings?

How do you navigate uncomfortable feelings?

MODULE THREE

Begin with the end in mind." In this section you will establish your vision. Imagining how the best version of you cares for you. Exploring how your life could look and feel differently if you were truly caring for yourself.

MODULE THREE

In this module you will learn:

- How to imagine the best version of you.

- Identify and understand your self-care barriers.

- Explore how your beliefs could be contributing to your lack of care.

- Notice body location for pleasant and unpleasant experiences.

- Explore when your thoughts, feelings, beliefs and actions reflect your best self.

Journal Time
IT'S HARD TO CARE FOR MYSELF BECAUSE

IMAGINE ME

"You've got to see it before you see it"

Create your best self prototype. What time do you wake up? When do your rest? What types of food do you eat? Who do you surround yourself with? What does your career and finances look like? What kind of spiritual practices do you engage in? Let your imagination do the work.

IMAGINE

REMEMBER

- This isn't about what you believe you can have it's about what you want.
- You get to explore what's important to you.
- Feel free to add more than what is listed above.
- Be as detailed as possible.
- Take 5 mins to visualize this person daily.

MY BEST SELF CARE

First think about the big picture of what you really want for your life. Think about how the best version of you cares for you. Jot down your best self, your barriers, and your beliefs.

MY BEST SELF...	MY BARRIERS...	MY BELIEF

BEING YOUR BEST SELF

Explore when you have shown up as your best self this week. Jot down what you were thinking, feeling, believing, and doing in the space below.

EXPLORE

- ☐ Your thoughts
- ☐ Your feelings
- ☐ Your beliefs
- ☐ Your actions

Staying connected to the best version of you.

▎ How can I connect with this version of me more often?

▎ How did I feel being the best version of me?

▎ When are some other times when I have been the best version of me?

YOUR DAY YOUR WAY

DAY 1 WEEK 3 ACTIVITY LOG

SELF-CARE IS NOT A *Last Resort*

Mark - or + for un/pleasant sensations

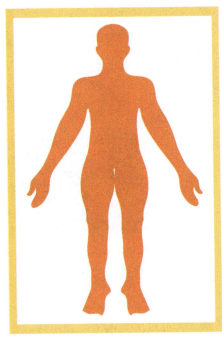

Rate your self-care 1-10

YOUR DAY YOUR WAY

DAY 2 WEEK 3 ACTIVITY LOG

Mark - or + for un/pleasant sensations

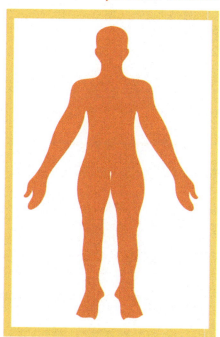

Rate your self-care 1-10

YOUR DAY YOUR WAY

DAY 3 WEEK 3 ACTIVITY LOG

Mark - or + for un/pleasant sensations

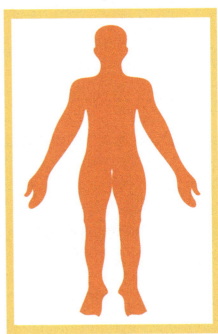

Rate your self-care 1-10

YOUR DAY YOUR WAY

DAY 4 WEEK 3 ACTIVITY LOG

Mark - or + for un/pleasant sensations

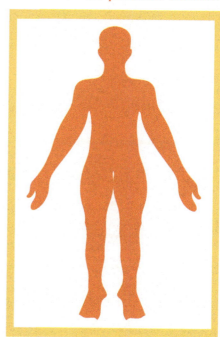

Rate your self-care 1-10

YOUR DAY YOUR WAY

DAY 5 WEEK 3 ACTIVITY LOG

SELF-CARE IS NOT A *Last Resort*

Mark - or + for un/pleasant sensations

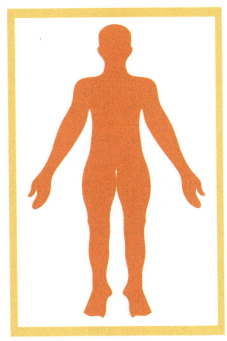

Rate your self-care 1-10

CULTIVATING CLARITY

Take some time and reflect over the past week. Ask yourself the following questions...

What have you noticed about your best self this week?

What experiences did you enjoy this week?

What activities did you find to be challenging?

What are your thoughts about the best version of you?

Where did your barriers and beliefs originate?

Which parts of your best self are your un/comfortable with?

MODULE FOUR

"If you fail to plan you plan to fail" In this Module you will identify how and when you will make time for self care. Schedule it on your calendar. Set a reminder in your phone. Grab an accountability partner.

MODULE FOUR

In this module you will learn:

- How to create S.M.A.R.T goals.

- Check your S.M.A.R.T goals with 2.0.

- Explore history related to inability and ability to follow through.

- How to be aware of your distractions.

- Identify accountability partners.

Journal Time
WHAT HAS BEEN YOUR GREATEST ACCOMPLISHMENT?

THE POWER OF A PLAN

S.M.A.R.T Goals

S.M.A.R.T Goals 2.0

BE S.M.A.R.T

SMART GOALS ARE

- [ ] Specific
- [ ] Measurable
- [ ] Attainable
- [ ] Realistic
- [ ] Time Oriented

Write out a specfic goal that you can measure. Choose something that you can attain in a realistic amount of time.

S.M.A.R.T CHECK

CHECK THE "WHY" OF YOUR GOAL

- [ ] Significant
- [ ] Meaningful
- [ ] Ambitious
- [ ] Relevant
- [ ] Time Sensitive

Write out why this goal is significant. What makes it meaningful to you? How does this goal activate your ambition? Be real about what you desire and be sensitive to time.

- _____
- _____
- _____
- _____
- _____

S.M.A.R.T SELF CARE

GOAL	STEPS TO MAKE IT HAPPEN	DEADLINE	✓
	....		

GOAL	STEPS TO MAKE IT HAPPEN	DEADLINE	✓
	....		

GOAL	STEPS TO MAKE IT HAPPEN	DEADLINE	✓
	....		

S.M.A.R.T SELF CARE

GOAL	STEPS TO MAKE IT HAPPEN	DEADLINE	✓
	....		

GOAL	STEPS TO MAKE IT HAPPEN	DEADLINE	✓
	....		

GOAL	STEPS TO MAKE IT HAPPEN	DEADLINE	✓
	....		

SELF CARE HATERS

Let's face it, we all have had some experience with a hater. Even if the hater is within us. Haters don't want you to succeed. On this worksheet you will get curious about your self care haters.

Question 1
Explore the last time you tried to engage in some form of self care. What hindered you from fully caring for yourself?

_____
_____
_____
_____
_____

Question 2
What would you consider to be a distraction? Explore what consumed your mental and physical space when trying to care for yourself?

_____
_____
_____
_____
_____

Question 3
Do you believe you deserve to be cared for? Why or why not?

_____
_____
_____
_____
_____

YOUR CIRCLE

Consider the top 6 people you communicate and interact with daily. How do you feel about those relationships? How do you feel around them? Do you feel motivated, inspired, fulfilled and cared for? Do these individuals inspire you, encourage you, and support your development?

1.
2.
3.
4.
5.
6.

YOUR IDEAL CIRCLE

Consider the top 6 people you would like to have in your circle. What attributes do they have? What do you need from these individuals? What can you offer these individuals? How do you want to feel around them? How do you imagine they can support you as you care for yourself?

1.

2.

3.

4.

5.

6.

YOUR DAY YOUR WAY

DAY 1 WEEK 4 ACTIVITY LOG

SELF-CARE IS HOW YOU COMMUNICATE

Your Standards

CHECK IN ON YOUR GOAL DAILY

Specific

Measurable

Attainable

Realistic

Time Sensitive

Rate your self-care 1-10

YOUR DAY YOUR WAY

DAY 2 WEEK 4 ACTIVITY LOG

SELF-CARE IS HOW YOU COMMUNICATE
Your Standards

CHECK IN ON YOUR GOAL DAILY

Specific

Measurable

Attainable

Realistic

Time Sensitive

Rate your self-care 1-10

YOUR DAY YOUR WAY

DAY 3 WEEK 4 ACTIVITY LOG

SELF-CARE IS HOW YOU COMMUNICATE

Your Standards

CHECK IN ON YOUR GOAL DAILY

Specific

Measurable

Attainable

Realistic

Time Sensitive

Rate your self-care 1-10

YOUR DAY YOUR WAY

DAY 4 WEEK 4 ACTIVITY LOG

SELF-CARE IS HOW YOU COMMUNICATE

Your Standards

CHECK IN ON YOUR GOAL DAILY

Specific

Measurable

Attainable

Realistic

Time Sensitive

Rate your self-care 1-10

YOUR DAY YOUR WAY

DAY 5 WEEK 4 ACTIVITY LOG

SELF-CARE IS HOW YOU COMMUNICATE

Your Standards

CHECK IN ON YOUR GOAL DAILY

Specific

Measurable

Attainable

Realistic

Time Sensitive

Rate your self-care 1-10

CULTIVATING CLARITY

Take some time and reflect over the past week. Ask yourself the following questions...

What have you noticed about your goals this week?

What activities did you enjoy this week?

What activities did you find to be challenging?

What are your thoughts about your circle?

What did you think about creating your Ideal Circle?

How do you plan to navigate your self-care Haters?

MODULE FIVE

"Time time for some time for some for some action" Now you have the green light. It's time to put it all together. Start engaging in this long awaited self care practices. Try something new make you a priority!

Journal Time
WRITE ABOUT A TIME WHEN YOU FELT CARED FOR?

MODULE FIVE

In this module you will learn:

- How to care for yourself utilizing senses.

- How to intergrate self-care into your daily life.

- The benefits of mindfulness.

- Your self care developmental stage.

- How to cultivate what you already have.

FIVE SENSES SELF CARE

Use your senses as a guide to enhance your self care practices.

- [ ] **Sight**
  Identify things you like to see, such as scenery, movies, pictures.

- [ ] **Sound**
  Identify things you enjoy hearing such as the ocean, rain, music, nature, traffic, laughter.

- [ ] **Touch**
  Identify what you like to feel. Explore textures, movements, temperatures and body positions.

- [ ] **Smell**
  Identify what you like to smell. Lavender, vanilla, citrus, clean fresh scents, or various foods.

- [ ] **Taste**
  Identify what you like to taste. Mint, sweet, salty and incorporate textures and temperatures such as cold, crunchy, soft, and warm.

MINDFULNESS EVERYDAY

Mindfulness is simply the act of being aware continuously and consistently.
What were you mindful of this week?

P.L.E.A.S.E	
PAUSE	MON
LISTEN	TUE
EXPERIENCE	WED
AWARENESS	
SENSE	THU
ENJOY	FRI
	SAT
	SUN

DEVELOPMENTAL STAGES OF SELF CARE

OBJECTIVES

- Understand stages.
- Identify your stage.
- Explore how to mature.

In this section we will explore your ***"Self-Care Developmental Stage (SCDS)"***

Newborn

Toddler

School Age

Adolescent

Adult

Elderly

DEVELOPMENTAL STAGES OF SELF CARE

Identify your developmental stage. Know that you may find yourself in more than one.

NEWBORN

Cries in hopes that someone else will meet their needs.
No cry, no care.
"If they don't give it to me, I won't have it.."

_____
_____
_____
_____

TODDLER

Curiosity discovering likes and dislikes. Just learning to use the word "NO".
Some fits and tantrums.
"I need you to tell me what I need".

_____
_____
_____
_____

SCHOOL AGE

Starting to understand who you are in relation to others. Aware of needs but feels guilty for asking for it.
"I feel sad when others don't want to play with me"

_____
_____
_____
_____

ADOLESCENT

Individualistic focus. Primarily concerned with their feelings.
My feelings are most important.
Fixed mindset.
"I know what I like so sucks for you"

_____
_____
_____
_____

ADULT

Mature Logical.
Aware of needs in every area.
Open to change, able to pivot.
"I can prioritize and prepare for self care."

_____
_____
_____
_____

ELDER

Wisdom. Acceptance of care from others. Recognize shift in needs. Understanding of the need to evolve. Ability to care for self and others simultaneously.

_____
_____
_____
_____

USE WHAT YOU HAVE

Identify 12 things you do on a daily, weekly, monthly, or yearly basis. How can these tasks or activities be categorized as self-care?

YOUR DAY YOUR WAY

DAY 1 WEEK 5 ACTIVITY LOG

SELF-CARE IS
A Process

Circle the types of self care you engaged in today.

NEWBORN

TODDLER

SCHOOL AGE

ADOLESCENT

ADULT

ELDER

Rate your self-care 1-10

YOUR DAY YOUR WAY

DAY 2 WEEK 5 ACTIVITY LOG

SELF-CARE IS

A Process

Circle the types of self care you engaged in today.

NEWBORN

TODDLER

SCHOOL AGE

ADOLESCENT

ADULT

ELDER

Rate your self-care 1-10

YOUR DAY YOUR WAY

DAY 3 WEEK 5 ACTIVITY LOG

SELF-CARE IS

A Process

Circle the types of self care you engaged in today.

NEWBORN

TODDLER

SCHOOL AGE

ADOLESCENT

ADULT

ELDER

Rate your self-care 1-10

YOUR DAY YOUR WAY

DAY 4 WEEK 5 ACTIVITY LOG

SELF-CARE IS

A Process

Circle the types of self care you engaged in today.

NEWBORN

TODDLER

SCHOOL AGE

ADOLESCENT

ADULT

ELDER

Rate your self-care 1-10

YOUR DAY YOUR WAY

DAY 5 WEEK 5 ACTIVITY LOG

SELF-CARE IS

A Process

Circle the types of self care you engaged in today.

NEWBORN

TODDLER

SCHOOL AGE

ADOLESCENT

ADULT

ELDER

Rate your self-care 1-10

CULTIVATING CLARITY

Take some time and reflect over the past week. Ask yourself the following questions...

What have you noticed about yourself this week?

What senses activity did you enjoy this week?

How can you be mindful of your preferred senses daily?

What are your thoughts concerning your SCDS?

How can you mature in your SCDS?

In what ways are you growing to care for yourself more?

MODULE SIX

"You can't lose if you learn" Now is the time for reflection. Be honest with yourself about how you feel. What did you enjoy the most. What did you find difficult. Do you need to continue with the same process or might it be beneficial to pivot. This is your strategy it's ok to take your time.

MODULE SIX

In this module you will:

- Utilize The Priority Matrix.

- Create Individual Compassion Phrases.

- Explore Whole Person Self-Care Ideas.

- The S.A.F.E Method.

- Reflect On Your Process and Your Progress.

Journal Time

HOW HAS YOUR PERSPECTIVE OF SELF CARE CHANGED?

SELF CARE PRIORITY MATRIX

Use this chart to prioritize your needs and various tasks.

	URGENT	NOT URGENT
IMPORTANT	DO it today	SCHEDULE a time to do it
NOT IMPORTANT	DELEGATE it	ELIMINATE it

STAY S.A.F.E

Practical way to helping you make self-care a priority.

I think we all can relate to starting something and becoming inconsistent over time. It is my hope that your self-care practices will last. The S.A.F.E approach is a way to keep self-care in the forefront of your mind.

SHARE SOME COMPASSION STATEMENTS BELOW:

- Say it
- Affirm it
- Feel it
- Embrace it

SELF-CARE IDEAS

Need some help? Here are a few options for self care.

SPIRITUAL

- [ ] PRAY
- [ ] MEDITATE
- [ ] COMMUNE
- [ ] GRATTITUDE
- [ ] EXPERIENCE NATURE

MENTAL

- [ ] READING
- [ ] PUZZLES
- [ ] PAINTING
- [ ] ASSEMBLING
- [ ] DIY PROJECTS
- [ ] LEARN NEW THINGS
- [ ] PLAY GAMES
- [ ] RESEARCH
- [ ] THERAPY
- [ ] SUPPORT OTHERS

PHYSICAL

- [ ] WALK
- [ ] DANCE
- [ ] YOGA
- [ ] SEX
- [ ] NAP
- [ ] HYDRATE
- [ ] DECLUTTER/CLEAN
- [ ] SHOWER/BATH
- [ ] SKIN CARE/MAKE-UP
- [ ] NOURISHING MEAL

FINANCIAL

- [ ] BUDGET
- [ ] SAVE
- [ ] INVEST
- [ ] PAY BILLS TIMELY
- [ ] CHARITABLE

EMOTIONAL

- [ ] THERAPY
- [ ] JOURNAL
- [ ] WRITING STORIES
- [ ] POETRY
- [ ] BOUNDARIES
- [ ] PETS
- [ ] SUPPORT SYSTEM
- [ ] CREATIVE DANCE
- [ ] SCREAM
- [ ] COMPASSION
- [ ] AFFIRMATIONS
- [ ] GARDENING

DAILY

- [ ] DIAPHRAM BREATHING
- [ ] BELLY LAUGHS
- [ ] SMILE

REFLECTION

Take a moment to reflect over the past 6 weeks. Review your original intentions. How do you feel about this experience? What have your learned about yourself? How have you grown? I hope you are proud of yourself. I am very proud of you!

YOUR DAY YOUR WAY

DAY 1 WEEK 6 ACTIVITY LOG

SELF-CARE LOOKS
Good on you

Circle the types of self care you engaged in today.

REMEMBER TO

BREATHE

LAUGH

SMILE

Rate your self-care 1-10

YOUR DAY YOUR WAY

DAY 2 WEEK 6 ACTIVITY LOG

SELF-CARE LOOKS
Good on you

Circle the types of self care you engaged in today.

REMEMBER TO

BREATHE

LAUGH

SMILE

Rate your self-care 1-10

YOUR DAY YOUR WAY

DAY 3 WEEK 6 ACTIVITY LOG

SELF-CARE LOOKS
Good on you

Circle the types of self care you engaged in today.

REMEMBER TO

BREATHE

LAUGH

SMILE

Rate your self-care 1-10

YOUR DAY YOUR WAY

DAY 4 WEEK 6 ACTIVITY LOG

SELF-CARE LOOKS

Good on you

Circle the types of self care you engaged in today.

REMEMBER TO

BREATHE

LAUGH

SMILE

Rate your self-care 1-10

YOUR DAY YOUR WAY

DAY 5 WEEK 6 ACTIVITY LOG

SELF-CARE LOOKS
Good on you

Circle the types of self care you engaged in today.

REMEMBER TO

BREATHE

LAUGH

SMILE

Rate your self-care 1-10

WRITE THE VISION

Now envision your next year. For each of the boxes below think about your goals and how you envision each of the aspects listed. Think about the WHY behind each of the goals and make sure they're driven by genuine intentions. Notice if there are words or mantras that jump out at you for this next year. How will your self care improvements impact the following areas next year?

BUSINESS

FITNESS

RELATIONSHIPS

FINANCIAL

EXPERIENCES

MINDSET

CHECK OUT

Now that you have completed this course I want you to do a quick self evaluation. Rate your present self care practices below. Remember No Shade, No Shame, No Blame, Just Reflect.

RATING SCALE

0 RARELY TRUE   **1** SOMETIMES TRUE   **2** OFTEN TRUE

1. I feel confident in my daily self-care practice. _____
2. I have a tendency to care for others before myself. _____
3. I have a tendency to ignore my personal needs. _____
4. I feel tired on most days. _____
5. When my day is complete I feel fulfilled. _____
6. I can recognize how and when to set boundaries. _____
7. I have a tendency to overextend myself. _____
8. I feel satisfied with the reciprocity in my relationships. _____
9. When I am overwhelmed I ask for help. _____
10. I feel guilty when I can't show up for others. _____

CONGRATULATIONS

You have successfully completed your self-care strategy!
Know that the work you have done is not at all easy.
It is my hope that you find that it was worth it.

AUTHOR   BUSINESS OWNER   BOUNDARIES COACH

Author Bio

Yunetta Spring Smith is a Thriving Therapreneur (Therapist + Entrepreneur) CEO and founder of Spring Forth Counseling and Ground Breakers Coaching & Consulting. She is a Licensed Professional Clinical Counselor in the State of TN, KY, and ID, as well as, a Nationally Certified, Counselor, Clinical Trauma Professional, and EMDR Therapist/Approved Consultant. Yunetta specializes in helping members of the BIPOC community navigate childhood trauma that manifests in adulthood. Working exclusively with public figures, professionals, pastors, and practitioners, she works diligently to spread awareness through various media platforms including, the weekly "Talk it out Tuesday" Segment on the Rickey Smiley Morning Show and Co-Host for the "Deeper than the Diet" Podcast. Yunetta is a ground breaker, stigma breaker, and a cycle breaker who cultivates spaces for healing, wholeness, compassion, and change. It is her hope that you will EMBRACE taking off your mask, EMBODY standing in your truth, and EXPERIENCE loving what you see!

THERAPIST   CONSULTANT   SELF-CARE STRATEGIST

LET'S STAY CONNECTED

MAILING ADDRESS
P.O Box 3801
Clarksville TN 37043

PHONE NUMBER
931-338-8882

EMAIL ADDRESS
GroundBreakersc.c@gmail.com

WANT TO JOIN THE MAILING LIST
TEXT "SPRING" TO 55444

WANT TO JOIN THE SELF CARE MASTER CLASS
TEXT "WELL" TO 33777

TWITTER
@yunettaspring

FACEBOOK
@springforthcounseling
@yunettaspring

INSTAGRAM
@springforthcounseling
@yunettaspring
@groundbreakerstherapy

YOUTUBE
@yunettaspring

Made in the USA
Columbia, SC
17 May 2022